Grass, AND
Letter in April

Also by Inger Christensen

AVAILABLE FROM NEW DIRECTIONS

alphabet

Azorno

Butterfly Valley: A Requiem

it

Light, Grass, AND *Letter in April*

BY INGER CHRISTENSEN

TRANSLATED FROM THE DANISH BY
SUSANNA NIED

DRAWINGS BY
JOHANNE FOSS

A NEW DIRECTIONS BOOK

Grateful acknowledgment is made to the editors of the following journals in which some of these poems originally appeared: *Poetry*, *Two Lines*, and *Scandinavian Review*.

The Publisher thanks Anders Sune Berg for photographing Johanne Foss's drawings.

This edition of *Light, Grass, and Letter in April* was published with the assistance of the Danish Literature Centre.

Book design by Sylvia Frezzolini Severance
Manufactured in the United States of America
First published as a New Directions Paperbook (NDP1187) in 2011.
Published simultaneously in Canada by Penguin Books Canada Limited
New Directions Books are printed on acid-free paper.

Library of Congress Cataloging-in-Publication Data
Christensen, Inger, 1935–2009.
[Poems. English. Selections]
Light, Grass, & Letter in April / by Inger Christensen ; translated from the Danish by Susanna Nied ; drawings by Johanne Foss.
p. cm.
ISBN 978-0-8112-1869-6 (acid-free paper)
1. Christensen, Inger, 1935–2009—Translations into English. I. Nied, Susanna.
II. Foss, Johanne. III. Title.
PT8176.13.H727A2 2011
839.81'174—dc23

2011018404

The translator is grateful to Peter Borum, Johanne Foss, Birgit Olsen, and Anne-Charlotte Hanes Harvey for their help with these translations, and to Declan Spring, editor par excellence.

10 9 8 7 6 5 4 3 2 1

New Directions Books are published for James Laughlin
by New Directions Publishing Corporation,
80 Eighth Avenue, New York 10011

Table of Contents

Introduction

*A*grandfather clock hovers in darkness over a snowy town. Near the pendulum, two lovers embrace; from the clock's side, a feathery wing extends. This is Marc Chagall's *Clock with Blue Wing*, which Inger Christensen touches and transmutes in the six-line poem that opens *Light*:

> If I stand
> alone in the snow
> it is clear
> that I am a clock
>
> how else would eternity
> find its way around

Light (*Lys*, 1962), the first of Christensen's six volumes of poetry, is bound here with *Grass* (*Græs*, 1963), her second volume, and *Letter in April* (*Brev i april*, 1979), her fourth. Through each volume readers can walk a little farther with Christensen as she lets eternity find its way.

Light and *Grass*, published only a year apart, may have more in common than have any of Christensen's other books. Both predate her use of complex structural systems, yet both move in increasingly experimental directions. Christensen's trademark penchant for innovative structure appears and evolves, along with her affinity for the natural world and her impulse toward synthesizing language, visual arts, and music. These poems show us the Danish landscapes that Christensen felt so much a part of; the colors, lines, and forms of works by artists she admired (Chagall, Picasso, Jackson Pollock, Asger Jorn); and the music she heard in everything from daily speech to religious liturgy to the time announcement on the telephone. Rhyme, meter, pattern, and cadence drift in and out like tides. At her early readings Christensen sang some of these poems to her own melodies, accompanied by avant-garde music. Her lifelong themes are already evident: boundaries between self and other, between human beings and the world; our longing and struggle for direct connection beyond boundaries; the roles of language and writing as mediators of that connection; the distances between words and the phenomena that they stand for.

In a 1984 newspaper interview, Christensen reflected on *Light* and *Grass*:

> The structure of a work of art isn't usually seen as a type of philosophy. But that's how I think of it, and I believe it's been that way for me since my first book was published. It was inherent in the poetic modernism of the period. In the minuscule linguistic universe that can be created in a poem, words and images follow each other so closely that everything comes to the surface. It's like a painting where one color is here and another color is there and nothing can be taken away without everything falling apart. The exactness needed within such a small network of relationships made writing interesting. I enjoyed keeping words and phenomena in suspension in relation to each other, experiencing

the way one can't hold them in one's thoughts simultaneously, yet can't keep them separate either."
—Erik Skyum-Nielsen interview, 1984, *Information*

The poems in *Light* and *Grass* do spring from the poetic modernism of their period—the mid-twentieth century—but they're going somewhere else. With the 1969 publication of Christensen's 230-page blockbuster *det* (*it*, New Directions, 2006), that "somewhere else" became clear. Blending mathematics and linguistics, encompassing the fury and hope of Europe's 1968 youth revolution in the face of the sociopolitical realities of the time, Christensen's outrageous, tender, demanding *it* bridged modernism and postmodernism, helping to catapult European poetry into a new era.

It was not until a decade later that her next volume of poetry, *Letter in April*, appeared. A complex fusion unique among Christensen's works, *Letter in April* is as quiet and understated as *it* is bold and broad.

The *Letter in April* poems were written in collaboration with graphic artist Johanne Foss, who began their project with a series of charcoal-on-parchment drawings of Etruscan artworks and places. "The violent elements of Etruscan art fascinated me in those days," Foss recalls. Christensen and Foss had known each other for several years. Both had stayed, at one time or another, in an artists' residence (San Cataldo) near Amalfi, Italy. Both had explored Etruscan ruins. Both had studied the Etruscan collection at Copenhagen's Ny Carlsberg Glyptotek museum. Christensen, taken by Foss's images of things they both knew well, chose a set of drawings from the series and began a manuscript in response to them, folding the images into her writing. Foss continued to create drawings, feeding them to Christensen as they were completed.

Over the next two years, the project progressed. During the summer months, Christensen and Foss worked from a country house in southern Sweden while their children played together, the days long and light, wood anemones carpeting the forest. During the rest of the year, they worked at their homes in Copenhagen—again, while their children played. From her father, a tailor, Christensen had inherited a sewing machine and innumerable spools of colored thread. The children would festoon the rooms with thread, weaving it into multicolored webs and mazes, as Christensen wrote, weaving together elements of her life and the philosophical, metaphysical, linguistic, and semiotic strands that have consistently informed her work. (Note her incorporation of Heidegger's concept of worldlessness into *Letter in April*, as well as her focus on sign systems: "Tell me / that things / speak their own / clear language.")

Christensen initially created a prose draft but discarded it, dissatisfied. She began again. This time a poetry manuscript emerged, a slender ribbon of short lines and simple words in verbal and visual counterpoint to Foss's drawings. Of course, the poems' apparent simplicity is deceptive. Set against the lions, gorgons, shadow landscapes, and grave mounds of an Etruscan netherworld, the poems wind inward, tracing an archetypal descent into a darkness where language itself fails, a labyrinth with a monster at its core. Yet the images also include the trees, fruits, and flowers of a timeless Italian summer. And the poems turn, winding back outward again, following their threads away from the labyrinth and toward everything that has been in place all along: the natural world; the languages, spoken and unspoken, of everyday tasks—the sign systems of child-rearing, daily errands, living as one human among others—a rebirth into light. The white anemones of northern forests appear, as do the children's thread mazes, innocuous toy labyrinths as easy to navigate as any plaything.

At another level, a more prosaic journey goes on in *Letter in April*. A woman travels with a child to a foreign country, where the two set up housekeeping for a few weeks. They experiment with a new language, meals are prepared, daily shopping is done, playgrounds are visited, excursions are made. Inger Christensen actually did travel with her young son to France to complete *Letter in April*. As she edited and interwove the poems, images from that real-life journey found their way into the manuscript as well, adding still another dimension to the duality of inner and outer worlds.

In the complex but subtle structure of *Letter in April* duality also plays a role. There are seven main sections, marked by Roman numerals I through VII. Each main section contains five subsections, marked with small circles o through ooooo, and arranged in varying order.

Section I:	ooooo, oooo, o, oo, ooo
Section II:	ooo, oo, ooooo, oooo, o
Section III:	o, oooo, ooo, oo, ooooo
Section IV:	ooooo, oo, o, oooo, ooo
Section V:	ooo, oooo, ooooo, oo, o
Section VI:	o, oo, ooo, oooo, ooooo
Section VII:	ooooo, oooo, o, oo, ooo

Subsections with the same number of small circles have motifs in common. The double structure of sections and subsections allows the book to be read in two ways. One can read straight through I–VII, in order. Or one can read I o, II o, III o . . . ; then I oo, II oo, III oo . . . ; then I ooo, II ooo, III ooo . . . and so on. The text is flexible enough that either grouping of the poems can work.

This structural flexibility arises not only from the subsections' shared motifs, but also from Christensen's instincts for mathematics and music. During the early 1970s she developed an interest in the work of French composer Olivier Messiaen (1908–1992), a pioneer of serialism. This innovative approach to tonality relies on individual notes organized into a set, or series, that involves no guiding chord. Mathematical patterns of permutation, as opposed to a central chord, guide variations within the given series of notes, producing unified compositions that circumvent traditional tonal harmony. Christensen found literary possibilities in serialist techniques. In *Letter in April*, she applies mathematical patterns of permutation to create a regular system of variations in the order of the subsections. As she had done for *it*, and as she later would do in an entirely different way for her 1981 *alfabet* (*alphabet*, New Directions, 2001), Christensen was able to convert mathematical principle into poetry—a poetry both visionary and grounded in the natural world, consistently transcending its own mathematical structures.

Letter in April is duality upon duality: in its visual/verbal genesis, in its musical/mathematical structures, and in its layered content incorporating the metaphysical within the prosaic. Fittingly, its first two pages also function as a double dedication. From poet to artist, a nuanced eight-line inscription in honor of their friendship and collaboration, ". . . our work with images, words, to bring all things back to the landscape they come from." From artist to poet, a delicate line of wildflowers from the hills of Italy.

SUSANNA NIED

Light

If I stand
alone in the snow
it is clear
that I am a clock

how else would eternity
find its way around

I tenderly lean toward night
with the aid of a rusty railing
find my way to my shoulder and cheek
find my way to my tenderness:
iron and flesh.

           The rest are banners
silently streaming, asking out and in,
in night-space, mind-space:

                      death?
lay my hand on the night's
trembling face,
pick bits of rust from my cheek.

What is my dead cracked body?
Ants in the snow have nothing to do.
No, my body is poetry, poetry.
I write it here: What is my body?
And the ants aimlessly move me
away, word by word, away.

In the wild loneliness of the mountains
I pull the pine-needle carpet
over me. Darkness
does not pause at the brink
presses with bristling needles
the unknown in me
opens opens

But do not grieve for me
do not grieve for your lonely
to and fro
My hour has rusted
My poem has left
your beaten track
Do not grieve My young poem
is more deeply kissed by life
Deathly it creeps
over under through me
Poetry is murdered hope.

Water surface
cuts itself
with ice

Winter boat
is frightened
ashore

Beneath the skin
a heart
guards itself

WINTER

Winter is out for a lot this year
the beach already is stiff
all will be one will be one this year
wings and ice will be one in the world
all will be changed in the world:
the boat will hear its steps on the ice
the war will hear its war on the ice
the woman will hear her hour on the ice
the hour of birth in the ice of death
winter is out for a lot.
Out for the houses the cities
out for the forests the clouds
the mountains the valleys fear
the heart the children peace.

Winter is out for a lot this year
the hand already is stiff
the crying of children is heard in the house
one we will be one life
I hear my house slip with the world
and scream all that has been screamed
the heart rams its boat into ice
shells rustling in the hull
winter is out for as much.

If I freeze fast in the ice
if you freeze fast my child
my great forest next summer

my great fear as I come
if you freeze fast my life:
then I am a vulture of wings and ice
tearing my liver, my living life
awake in eternity.

This winter is in for a lot.

SANDEMOSE

The sun hangs low in the little year
the bracken ponders darkness
the brave path has vanished
the great house is mere wood
in the paneling an enemy rustles

The chair gives you leave to sit
the table gives you leave to sit
the bread leaves you standing out
small grains of words
grains of bodies
grind and crush your hand
your soul
the enemy rustles

Letters ferment behind old paneling
flour mumbles in your mouth
the bark beetle runes itself a road
your brain blasts its time
the enemy is loose

The walls creep away
the tools creep away
the clock creeps to a stop
they have gone for a walk
your table and your chair

they brood over old
greedy words
high on the snow-white fell

You are on your way

ITINERARY

Everywhere a tiny straw
that floats away
pain portions out its color
on stones and fragile water
Everywhere a memory's last power:
where were we last year, now?
earth covers your brow?
you drowned . . . but here
we can rest, my dear
portion out time carefully
eat, sleep, see the sights . . . by-and-by
good old Europe! Perhaps!
but don't you forget the maps!
where did we go last summer?
tiny straw floats away.

TRANSIENCE

The stone on the beach evaporates.
The lake is gone in the sun.
Animals' desert skeletons
concealed in eternal sand.
Things wander,
die in each other,
sail like thoughts
in the soul of space.
Caravans of living sand.

Is this a threat?
Where is my heart?
Caught in the stone.
Concealed in a lake.
Beating deep
inside a humped camel
lying and groaning
and dying in sand.

SHOWER

Questioning
my eyes brush
nakedness
The mirror drips
down
from my feet
down
the rusty drain

FATHER—SON

I wish I could remember
whether I've done anything
the letter you received
was full of hidden meanings
the burning bush
did not burn me
this morning I got up too late

I wrote the letter
and never did send it
I lay at the stake
but never was burned
you sit in your chair
and nothing has happened

I wish I could remember
whether I've done anything

SORROW

Find the concise
expression for sorrow:
a slug with its slime
and reflex mechanism
in meaningless order,
the feelers out
in time, in time
drawn in again,
and inside the body
used precisely
as a pregnant siren
whose falling tone
falls and falls
down through all
organism.
Oh skin
my outermost
radar screen

Like a privateer
the fish flies out
and casts its fanfare-body
in an arc I fly
feel prey in my mouth
suck snakes' blood
spit more blood
my own
the prey of preys

MANIA

No land is there
not sleep's
not sorrow's

Walk and walk
along this railing
a balcony in space
no house, no garden

Count only
the red bars
count to the last

Death's land is there

I always thought reality
was something you became
when you grew up.

In the square stands Fata Morgana
looking tired, shouting
Morning paper — morning paper

An inner mumbling
squirms forward
walls drown
houses are lost
forests creep
over the earth.

I do not mumble
I will not
squirm forward.
I will not speak
of things
that are destroyed.

An inner mumbling
squirms forward
in us all.
Animals and people
are whirled along
through water.

What if
you have forgotten
the word
that parts
the waters
again.

It's very strange
the eggs are everywhere

There must be some mistake
the eggs are so close together

There seems to be no room for us
Push the eggs closer together

It's impossible
We must get closer together

but beloved what will happen
with all the eggs everywhere

what will happen everywhere
to us

There must be some mistake

Like slate-gray sea
my winter-flattened brain
sways in space

a flying lighthouse swings
my fall-eyes
around

what we called land
is the nearest stars

Weathered bramble
pricks my winter-
stiffened palm

bears me lightly
on its thorn
of orange blood

calls my gash
my dark time
into question

sets a timeless
seven-pointed
leaf on my soul

My convulsive hand
my bravery
my little stiffened
continental coast
missile–monologically
hardened
horrified
I will not move
come blue bird
I will not touch you
lay your deaf ear
to my sluggish pulse
I will do you
no more

Inflated, distended, wasted
or not yet totally lost
with the gray electrodes of the future
strapped onto memory's
faded fingertip
I stand and stammer
that I want to be good

CRUX

Spring tide switchblade
crux of the matter
in the perspective of the future
I your eyeservant see you,
spy on your extremes
your furious forays
against the coast of innocence
where the faithful live

Come little faith that thinks
that it all comes down to figures
your roomy statistics on sorrow
have in the final analysis figured
... the unfigurable
and on the whole as it has been
so it shall be and what we have received
we shall receive again in the course of time
when sooner or later
it converges again
and not even the beach can be seen

I hold myself still on the beach
lie in wait for what you call fate
lie like an old weathered stone
smiling nevertheless at the wave
Pious little faith that thinks
that I will keep a straight face
Under my skin you are already high tide

and treacherous ambush at night
hatred of my own future
and longing to be a knife
I am cold

I am cold on the beach   I am another
I carry stone   Strike water from my stone
but who can conjure up himself
who can leap over
who can throw the switchblade
so that it flies past
and the tidal wave no longer strikes
I am cold

Slice through then
strike the words together
about the unspeakable fact
that I am cold and afraid
and nevertheless lend
you flattery ears and eyes
to see unerringly
This is a closer coast
utterly false forgery
as when boiling sorrow
spews up useful wreckage
and the dead bare their lives:

I am the crux of the matter

Sitting on my little rational branch
sawing sawing with a rough rusty saw
a plaything saved since my childhood

sawing sawing winter's coming
hurry hurry eager hands
cast me cast me down to myself

I

> "A man and a woman
> Are one.
> A man and a woman and a blackbird
> Are one."

Feather-wrapped union
You and a blackbird's wing
Eveningtree's singing jewel
The man's camouflage in the bird
The bird's clear vision in him
Natural flight Consciousness
I
I am the one who is watching

Twilight of bliss
Man and blackbird defeated
The drive at rest in both
Drinking with one heart
Singing with one beak
Close-up of entrenchment
I
I am the one who is outside

Unreal pain
Blackbird's play and your voice
Relationship's echo and evening
Listening to the man's song

Grasping the bird's speech
Calling Am I a woman
I
I am the one who is open

MEN'S VOICES

Men's voices in the dark
—once in a temple—
men's voices in the sun
—once I was caryatid
number nine—
men's voices in the park
—I was a statue
untouchable naked
with no other mirror
than the fingers of the air
yielding to thought after thought
with no other sadness
than the rustling of leaves—
men's voices in the park:
why did they waken me?

CONSPIRACY

Bay clearly blue.
Victory completely certain.
Stones stone.
You gone.

Alone will stand with why
with blotched walls why
with the speed you drove into my heart
with the night I lay oblivion
under the volcano   raw

Whimper spit mock
you hate you why
sing dear sing why
eat lies think when
ink flows to oblivion
the fire dies the fire dies

A slope in the brain
a reaching for the ceiling
in empty houses

The grayworn wood
receives the body
absorbs blood

Expect me tonight
I know we cannot
make it. Coming.

The pupil that attracts you
the currents contoured
to the outline of the ocean floor
half-naked girl

Go on in
to her brain
put away your weapons
her body is a weapon

What you aim at yourselves
you aim at the ocean
It sees, sees

Wings surge above war
foreignness rises
distant burning doves
light up your skin

beautiful pure life: here
of sand and iron
compressed hope
glimpse bomb droplet

you   skin   dove

JELLYFISH

Clouds' wistfulness. Already a wintry light.
And summer's last suns driven up on the shore
blue-pale jellyfish on the sand.
I take them, slime-covered, cold, in my hand
stand with a flaccid sun under the sky—
seed slips between stiffened fingers.
I note the haphazardly sectioned design
mysterious unity of eyes and sex
a listening for other systems of suns.
Are you crying again. How scattered we are.
Longing to be identical again
to wander like burning sexes and suns
through the sky before everything darkens.
But the cloud drift has already stopped.
The jellyfish turn bluer still, frozen and small.
Summer's flight shut inside.
I stand with a flaccid sun under the sky:
oh to keep its fertile warmth for the winter.

DEEP WITHIN

Darkness gurgles through lungs and land
the wind turns known places trite
the place in the mouth where shouts stand in line
the place where hope will not die
bares us, silent, sluggish
in the world where everything counts
puts words in our mouths
that nothing counts

Darkness goes out and in through the head
nothing out, nothing in
trees branch in each branch of the blood
oxidize my unrest with night and wind
night and wind of nothing

I had better admit it now deep within
where you may be sitting behind the eye, thinking
that when we met and the sun and no end
I had better admit it now
that dark and evil, that night and I
that we that I and I
and ask

Darkness concentrates on the highest guardroom
the door to the brain has already been forced
what is it we have what is it we lack
what is it where are we what do we see
with a beacon's anguish, a beacon's anguish
what are we and to what do we cling
at sea two hearts with flares on board

BLUE POLES

Tonight, away begins to go
farther away, and the dream
what do we know of the dream
metallic leaps Jackson Pollock
silvery streams Jackson Pollock
I gaze across the sea

see in the distance your walk and you
pass the Pacific, distant and blue
phallus and Moloch pace my view
on into otherness

on into otherness?
are we in the world after or before
are we or are we not magnetic force
it is apparently me you inform:

genesis woman dream that begins
tonight to go farther away
tonight to reach farther away
metallic leaps Jackson Pollock
silvery streams Jackson Pollock
on across the blue sea

DAWN

Day ruffled
by wind one morning
owl feathers
in a lighter way
the mind changes
shrinks
something is gone

CITY OF MAN

When we get beneath the skin
when we get beneath the skin of the earth
when emptiness is not enough and the fever
          purifies a nothingness, a moment, tears
          and courage, shifting rain and rain
when we unfinished ones

When folly is foolish good
when the gutter boat sails and sails
          unknowing, ravaged
when the flesh is deeper.

Deeper the flesh and the wound and the city swallowed
          by the earth and without rest
Deeper the sickness rises in all
          sewers with sludge over
          loins and breasts and maimed
          eyes
Deeper distance-weakened, almost
          where the streets cross, loved.

The city where waterworks gurgle
          their evening of stubbornness we
          pour past
The city where the parsonage garden
          sighs its poplar faith
          leaf after leaf on
          the street that pours past

The city that pours us nearer ourselves
          and without rest

It is a city that sings in the heart
          when we get in
It is a city of man that lives
          beneath the skin where the battle is lost
It is a city with muffled faith
          and muffled rain deep under flesh

Be good, be good and without the hope
          of righteousness, a moment's
          earth
Be good and all those who sleep
          beneath us, shifting death
          and death
It is a city of love

Sudden red spot on my summer arm
childhood's patient fingertip angel
who flew to Our Lord and prayed for tomorrow

And good weather has suddenly come
good weather I hold in my hand
Lady Lady with child as you flew
tomorrow has come

If I carry you all the way home
my love will be red

You walk past me
as we sit completely still

I talk past myself
as you do not hear

We do nothing
and an angel gathers us up

LIGHT

I

Once more I recognize
a light within language
the closed words
that are there to be loved
and repeated until they are simple
A swan that folds itself
over the egg
is still an echo
of creation in us
And the swan flying
your eye toward the sun
is yet again harbinger
of wonder

We manage to recognize
light in the word
imperceptible act
from man to woman
A word that transforms
your mind to a swan
is simple enough
to give shape to an egg
And the language that shuts itself
into the egg
has wings that bear
from birth to light
And the sun is there to be loved

II

I think up a sun
a swan and madness
a material that glows
immaterially
that boundlessly swings
the lantern of chance
So tangible a wonder
is light
when eternity condenses
treads near
and does not kill

I think up a mask
of marbled sun
a guise of stiff feathers
and white substance in the brain
Let death be cold
I think up a wonder
that the heart is a lantern
swung by chance
between this self
and nothing
in madness and in light

III

I think a light
soberly I grasp
that the sun is stronger
the body's fall
the swirling flakes
of light around itself

I think a promise
on a par with purity
that light has given us
stronger wings
than the sun's in space
for this dying

And else just the body
sparingly lit
by its uncertain promise
never a wall
and only this ever:
I think a light

IV

Perhaps this growing
is the same
I think up a tree
imagination and a bird
and through all bounds
wings write
the growing dream
And where you fell
sleep has other depths
and opens winds
from what has been torn loose

I think up a sorrow
and where it fell
the bird has again
hung a nest
as big as the sky
for my mind to live in
Perhaps this growing
is the same
as living in the dream
No sorrow can prevent
imagination and bird

V

Repeat it to me
that this is enough
that this is the body's
cloud of light
that this is now

The dust has no
despairing echo
our only life
is a rose of life
which we love

Repeat it my love:
the lantern you swing
so soundlessly around me
is yet again
a child in its beginning

After the first morning I seek
the muted earthsmoke of language

Again and again I kiss the memory of
wake me! wake me! The sun and the swir-
ling wings in morning-bronze haze

What you gave my thoughts is the resistance
of the sting, hidden in my hovering
flower

What you gave me is pure morning

My passion: to awaken

In the brown hour
my love is green
on hard lava
sea grass, cool and long

The rest, the ocean's
distant song

HE

He is a tiny penny hidden
       in the wishing well of hope
He is the red in one morning's sun
       the color I last would lose
He is what I find early in
       early clover without seeking
He is a crack in winter earth
       stubborn springtime, watermouth
chuckling kisses

He is the strong exorcist of terror
       crying with a bird's consolation
He is the clay slope hardened
       by the sun's long battle with his body
       where pairs of swallows brood
He is in ticking wings the first
       meeting with morningblue air
He is in song and beak to beak

The earth catches its window, swings
       and creaks with time
The earth grips its bird and bricks it in
       with gray
The earth locks its wellspring
       into a bulletproof box
The earth devours the burning beak
       where the sunbird falls

I will not be ashamed
        of my hope in the dead
I will not be ashamed
        of my hope in the hope of him I love
I bear his mighty sunsong
        morning evanescent meeting
I open the window of my love
        inhale the smell of earth
        that is us
        and evanescent hope
which in spite of all
        we hope

Grass

PEACE

Doves grow in the field
From dust shalt thou again arise

GREEN

Green in green country
here the days come
closer to time
do not divide
but closer to sun
here no people
come forth
but lie in deep
grain and peace
and scent themselves closer
to yellow and blue
where a summer steeply rises
and deeply vanishes

BENEATH A TOWN

Beneath a town
the great course
that is not ours

Beneath a stone
the white roots
that bear us

When I look at the grass
I see uncertainty

Death with no direction
Life with no direction

In the grass children and birds

UNDER LAPWING-LAND'S CRY

Under lapwing-land's cry
    scurrying young
Under my wings
    children's fear
Under my wings
    yes and no

The beach repeats its tears
and joy flings itself away

WHISPERING GRASSFEET

Whispering grassfeet
steal through us
fir-fingers touch one another
where the paths meet
thick dripping resin
glues us together
summer-greedy woodpeckers
hammer at hardy
seed-hiding hearts

BY THE ROAD

Choosing acceptable knolls
for a short cigarette break.
Talking of birches' leaves
because it is birches we see.
Birches with fluttering leaves
along the white trunks.
Talking of other birches
with naked trunks.
Talking of years.
The space between us.
Maybe it's empty.

Seeing a group of children come up.
Hearing them ask the way.
Saying yes and seeing them run
embarrassed smiling run
in the right direction.
Crushing the cigarettes' glow
in the sand where they ran.
Trying to go on ourselves
— between us.

SEPTEMBER

Slowness dissolves
the still bench rejoices at last
women who knitted
      all summer together
look around
let stitches run
run in pure and simple excess
tears run
and are drops in the sea
children are born
          look around

TO GO IN

To go in without knowing it
To point at the door without knowing it
To go into the mountain and it is you
To go farther in and it is not certain
To go still farther in
and there is always room
and it is you they move
and it is always open
and it is you that is open
without knowing it endlessly open
They had lit a sun
They had raised a flag
To go farther in

WORDS

Words laid straight
after now and here

eyes in pain
as distance draws near

EACH ON YOUR OWN SEA

Each on your own sea
in your own depths
with your own pride
with flag and arms and mouth
and bravery's feather-decked horror
each with your own heart
each
your own

GRAY HAZE

Gray haze over Knebel Cove.
Hidden whirring knives.
In this almost random place
that touches me almost at random
Who is in power?

And beneath the water.
Beneath the same silicon-gray haze
that floats so deep in me.
Hidden whirring knives.
Who is not in power?

Powerless sandpipers—
Cutting cries—
Gray haze over Knebel Cove.

TURNING TO STONE

Over on the table
are my hands
Way down on the floor
are my feet
Far off
in some distant place
I do not see
what you see
with my eyes

SUSPENSE

I call to someone calling
the bridge is long and empty
Run out to reconcile
violent asphalt lights
springing aside
and swelling rails
on their way through my heart
I call to someone calling
someone calling . . .

LONGING

Betray myself
sit up nights
      burn candles
seek
seek with my hands
though I can see
find a crack in the wall
kiss you

TOGETHER

and footsteps behind me
back there
footsteps
I do not hear them
I walk
walk so thickly
            in a rain of tar
drag myself in
in toward the back
press my body
to the body of the house
stand
            with all that's crumbled
stuck tightly to my being

CONTACT

To sketch a spindly circle
in water or air
put a finger to my lips
and quiet the belief
put a hand to my heart
answer you honestly:
to answer nothing
wish nothing
defend your alien hand
with open arms
defend the weak
with faith
answer the strong
with faith
the strong and the weak
who all have alien hands
who all have alien hands
that are slowly moved and exchanged
the weak the strong
to answer you honestly
sketch a circle
in water or air

LOVING

Gathering wild strawberries
in a blackthorn thicket
easing my hand in
under far too early
fear and pain
handing you your heart
little child

SUMMERSHORT LIFE

Summershort life
lonely frost in flower
love's tree of stars

IS NO ONE COMING

Looking into the gossip mirror in there out there
        angled light opposite and red just creeping the tiny
        beetle reflectors away from away from
looking for you just if coming for whom by the way
        coming with tiny feelers without making it, shadow
hoping for water that will wash you home through air
        like a bath when I throw all windows out of our
        house
begging for wind that will pull your limbs you skin
        hair sex clearly playing in air when I turn off
        the radio now
removing the infected eyes and scratching my thoughts
        with the pencil no one must see for this is said
        and said in all confidential darkness this glimmer
        continues without eyes continues as with ant after
        ant finding nothing but ant after ant legions of
        blindness or what
what about the feeling of grass among ants in grass
        where we travel for years the grass where we lay
        coming creeping the children see see a flower from
        the holy place no not coming
is no one coming in angled light and forgotten through
        grass through sun without a mirror through eyes
        without ants through you
is no one coming through you?

OTHERWISE — TOUCHED BY LIGHT

Otherwise — touched by light we will get up
      throw all shimmers from our backs and stride
      like lions in grassgreen dark inevitable
      entrance
Houses do not worry us The nights flew with the
      dappled roof tiles threw the door into the sea
      where it floated why
To go in there and close it behind you not yet
      though deadly violence between far too many
      eyes could be avoided
precisely with the handle's pressure with downcast
      eyes slung between no expectations and sleep
      curlicues vis-a-vis what, with newspapers
      over their heads
untried the coffee and other overused stimuli deep-rooted
      signature dark as basalt on a large conjugal
      lifetime solitaire comes out comes out
no fortunately does not yet come out at all, nor
      come in, let the doors sail their open seas and
      let the nights plant our fragile mirrors in the
      ground over graves
here in a gentle intermezzo we stand and look at what
      it means to stand smiling for eternity in bright
      epitaphs and never again rise up with the
      grass after rain
but no not yet the morning wind unfolds all that's
      crumpled and stretches its whitest sunpaper up
      toward a crackling mad sky

flies in the face of the first the best who knows
	maybe me with my longstanding deep-rooted
	polishing complex my own little sparkling nail reflex
here where we file at the already bitten-off already
	bruised pettily vanished ones here where we are
	strong in the fear here
here steeply descending like
	death
	and closing our eyes with a snap
	across the mirror
	morning
then it is strangely far to the next one a hand comes
	creeping lays its goodness on the eyes body comes
	creeping melts our darkness with grass scent,
	folds us together
	against far too much behind us
aren't we ever going to then aren't we ever listen
	little lion never play solitaire but take me by
	the hand and pull me up
then you are strangely close to being here rolling
	in grass without relating to chairs wholly without
	knowledge of the word value or beds
Lions do not wear clothes in the grass
Lions do not wear mirrors on their foreheads
Lions have never even heard of ants
then you are strangely close to saying something
	besides roar in a glimmer of the windows'
	collected fear getting closer close to saying
	something besides roar in my mouth
in a glimmer of what on the edge of just now seeks

to be re-established with doors and roof tiles
facades of chairs and beds and contents of
mirrored conjugal cupboards because they are
going farther
all the glimmering houses are going farther
feinschmecker-correctly farther, nonskid
welfare-solitaire goes farther farther comes out
out out
strangely close to saying something else cross out
promise, promise nothing, just like that, don't
you think yes: lion and
otherwise risen in freed expression striding into
yourself through grass and in an entrance dark
you are close to a stronger light where the
words move like lions
Darkness!
come greatly where we came to love us awake
— with the grass one morning after rain

OTHERNESS TOUCHED

Otherness touched. Still with flecks of grass
        on sated skin as in silence

Still with leaves on hands and feet
        place as at last

Otherness at last. That changing
        to and from lasting place
        is here

Otherness that remembers your voice
        in gray-brown forest fungi

Sleep that in prickling needles remembers
        your body a sunfleck

Still with primal fog colors

Still with separate

Separate that leads you separate

Still with grass after grass

Into an otherness at last

as touched

MEETING

I

I fear the impersonal between us, things we cast off without
  tolerating or bearing, things whose stories we no longer
  try to remember, and roads that go round and round with-
  out anticipation

I fear the back, with a remnant of the pressure of metamor-
  phosis still under its skin, with little nervous lights still un-
  der closed eyelids, I fear the back

fear the clothes, the blankets, the closet door, everything that
  conceals, even with life, with small movements and open-
  ings in the flesh I fear the eyelid—won't open it wide, don't
  want to see the back, and don't want to see nothingness

I think we have sought wings on the back, I think we have
  sought light in the eyes, sought places, along roads, each
  other, God

this sloppy dishrag smack across the mouth, this vindictive face,
  the grin and slamming doors—the pupil that lies in wait
  in the dark and always claws the homecomer

this deep scratch in the throat, these shouts that repeat over-
  worked books rip them up with teeth without hunger and
  swallow these tasteless pills prozil niamid upharsin and
  mene mene nothing, while the moon-pot pours and bright
  greasy gravy oozes over everything

what does it want, this opening in the lap—what does this cloth
  dog of childhood want, always sitting up, with arms, star-
  ing

I fear this cloth dog, the picture on the wall of mother and child, Picasso's dove of peace bigger than the earth, the calendar with shiny pages looking at us, our fear and flight, when we sweat each by himself

I fear this opening in the lap, try to close it—everything is like cactus and stone and backs and wires that cannot reach

what is meeting, now when we light a cigarette and look back, now when eyes no longer wait to look into eyes, only now and then secretly examine the other, the beloved other stranger, run the vacuum cleaner, turn pockets inside out, look your fill at a yellow pimple, one hair out of place and never reach the eyes

what is meeting—someone is dead, long live someone, the living room is a full card file, streetcars with their backs lined up, tattered cardboard boxes filled with detritus from the most recent thoughts' move, what is meeting till death do us part

will we come out then—is there an opening, wire, switch, when we suddenly find, and wings shall bear all that we do not, and death shall have no dominion

but dream—God—what is meeting, I take this comb to comb his hair, but he has a comb there in his hand, he puts this apple in my lap, but I am so full, oh autumn, drawers and boxes and the closed cover of the radio, I wanted to seek

these roads, voices in the street like shining rails—who run into each other through the open jaws, is anyone left lying there, has everyone driven in, so the crane can swing them out over the edge

there should be a caution sign here, what does this death want before my eyes, why doesn't He turn his back, is he sick

I fear this sickness succeeding itself in us, this stinginess, the

smell of sweat, take it away, it isn't like mine, the glob of
phlegm in the wash basin, get it out—everything is catch-
ing, this Look what I'm giving you, so you'll never notice
what I'm taking—give us a smile, come on, a great big one
. . . ah, that was good, or the disappointment when it was-
n't very big, but it was your own damn fault honey

honey lights another cigarette, looks back and down at a little
dirt under her fingernails, fears the fine porcelain clock
where the swallows no longer tick and the tense two-way
switch that fills the whole living room, conducts the cur-
rent in separate directions, where we sit and cannot touch
each other

fears the rusty bicycles that pedaled to the beach once, the
dream again, yes but need, desire, and hope, wish, yes child-
ishness, now when the ashes are shoved under the door-
mat and the shoe polish is long since used up

so far the door is locked and no one knows whether we have
gone or come, whether this is a year or already the after-
time, what have you said to the others, to the men down
on the corner, is there a corner, to whom have I written
about my heart as if it were a question of feelings, did you
read it all in the paper, to whom

I fear the back, the back that answers all questions without
mouth or eyes, with a coffee can's dogged innocence and
the ironing board's cold shoulders

has something been hidden, what has been hidden, what lies
hidden in the old suitcase with tags to and from, to and
from whom, what lies concealed at the bottom of the dirty
clothes hamper stifled under the pressure of clammy and
greasy and crawling, though we do not have bugs, what is

there in the bedclothes, what lies concealed in my heart
don't stop, don't stop here, this obedient pumping, these long
    hauls, hoist me up, pull me in over the edge, the edge of
    the well, the box, whatever, the edge of the chair, like that,
    yes, a little more, no for God's sake *a lot* and hearing your
    voice: I think I'd like to sleep a little—or was it mine, what
    is meeting
I fear the impersonal between us, this shrugging of the shoul-
    ders, the back's grimaces, so long, so long, you don't mind
    that, do you, and don't worry about it, it doesn't mean any-
    thing—the priest with his back to the congregation, is it
    always God he sees, oh turn, turn around, say something
fear the old voices on the tape, no don't say anything, let us see,
    see, see each other and You
what have I said, suddenly asked, entreated, implored, begged—
oh this stubborn largish lump on the back, where the brain
    runs down into the backbone, pressure of metamorphosis,
    memory of salt on the lip after kissing, long stories, cre-
    ation, wind's confidences, the lap's wide opening
is someone coming toward me on the road
am I sitting with my face turned toward someone? R.S.V.P.

II

When morning stretches up again, when I again can touch the
    telephone and dial out into the air, this is seagull-wings—
    is that you yes screech and the daytime-windows open dis-
    tant all political unrest

there are still twelve gold-rusty asters left, one I found be-
    witched sailing in the washbasin, water-wakening miracle,
    who was wakened—and one lay face-down, close to the
    newspaper stack, bled

twelve are left on the table full as if unfolded, what will be-
    come of approaching unrest the buds the hours' spring-
    board and amount to something as if in one big blossom-
    ing

I remember a black man's song that stripped all skin like hate
    from our bodies, remember the gold-rust of his voice's in-
    sanity-pump where water was soft as children and the air-
    knife hard as sun

remember that the day has begun, this day, when yesterday's
    dress is locked in the closet, the telephone book hidden
    under the bed and the map of this metropolis need not be
    used to get through again and again in vain

this day that holds the restless night in its hand like a shriveled
    berry, a crumpled dial, will not use you any longer, this
    zero zero five five just to hear a voice and what a voice,
    Time, preacher without illusions 1:45:16 beep again and
    again 2–3–4 something or other beep and sleep

this day light the torch and pass it to one in chains melt his fear
    which is mine with faith, throw the bread up high, let it
    fly around the world and fall like manna on the strangers,

wing-bread here—is that you yes screech and fill us up
with your faith

oh germinal vision give them grain bread bread, oh approach-
ing unrest go away fill yourself with bread bread, strip from
us layer after layer of furs, crazy jewels and books, I mean
paper, this bright paper industry, this formless overgrown
baby crying more and more with its several hundreds of
years—strip from us layer after layer of the mind's con-
scious wanderings farther and farther out but in ever
smaller circles—strip this poem of everything—grind it,
mill it, flour, bread, faith

this poem—why don't I stop, you stand by my side conjuring
smiles, don't I understand even a smattering of the
whole—my poem which you will never see smatter smat-
ter—oh European times of beep beep beep, while the
black man sings, smiles smiles smiles

this poem this day if you stop the poem, you stop the day, this
poem draws nearer, seagull-wings, yes, speaking, who's
this—have you already risen from the ashes my love of
course I have the coffee ready

these words we say, be careful, still a bit of gold-rust which must
not lose its value, still the long stalks in water when the stom-
ach sinks, the opening, the faith must never be closed

if you come like this and I come like this, with our backs to all
the hangovers of the past, overgrown hearts beat in our
bodies, fill our chests, stomachs, bulge from our backs, as if
far too much were included—grind it, heart! new, steam-
ing bread, daytime, still twelve asters and aftertime of the
miracle

meeting is always face-on

III

I do not know what it is. I cannot tell you what it is. I have no
 clear concept; as with words, it is no longer clear what they
 are.

Within the world. Once lost in the grass and always happily
 crawling. One second the connection with evil lost and
 always thoughts about some little approaching second or
 other.

Care only about trees. They open out, fold in, close, stand ajar.
 They have a tree-life, longer on the average. Trees are also
 beautiful.

Care only about sea and sky and earth. The streaming, lifting,
 bearing. The longest-living and all that moves with, in, on;
 it is no longer clear what it is.

But it is within the world. We have stood up somewhere and
 begin with steps. We press close to a tree to remember the
 grass. We press close to each other to remember the tree.
 Step by step we go farther, try to remember the body, press
 close to the wind and to space to try to see what it is.

But it is no longer clear. We are within the world. Grass, tree,
 body. Sea, sky, earth—care only about those. Nothing has
 happened. But there is a silence. There is a lie. I cannot say
 what it is.

Time sneaks kindly about. Streets blossom. Houses sway like
 palms. Seagulls circle the holy flagpole. Everything is in vi-
 olent upheaval, like flowered dresses on tourist boats. I have
 no clear concept. But bravely we say hello and goodbye or
 lay wreaths.

My love—for that word exists—there is a lie. There is a closed door. I can see it. It is gray. It has a little black hand to shake hello and goodbye. It has a little, black, stiff hand, which is completely still now. That door is not a lie. I sit and stare at it. And it is not a lie. I cannot tell you what it is.

IV

As we touched each other before, it was death we touched

as we pulled and pulled, each on his own side of the door, it
was death we held fast

held each other fast to the very end, closing time and no de-
liveries, pain

until the door loosened its grip on us, opened up to us and saw
that we were gone

I fear this poem which is like a procession word after word
with their endings gone, what then?

this lie that we enter with leaf-fingers, grain-hair and flower-
breath, arms like lilies and bodies like swaying birches and
all that is fair in the world and suddenly faded

this lie that we enter again with the certainty of a lie: Laugh,
little children, like scythe after grain and eventually age in
young and old's favor and clap your small hands for as long
as you can

what then? I could address you, my love, write a letter from a
place, maybe even from a real place, if there is such a thing,
before dinnertime

oh world-place here, where it all could be born, bear with my
unrest, see the old wooden table with things that go to or
fro, it needs polishing, pull open the curtains, but it is night

it is night, the window-rain glistens especially courteously, out-
side hurries home on the bus for the redeemed, who know
where they are going

to a place, maybe, a real place

more and more to remember, this meeting you mentioned to-
day when we saw each other occurred precisely today

when we saw each other, just remind me of that

I hear them talk in the street; perhaps it is happiness talking, without this dull procession of words, stammering in sovereignty like rain and wind

here I must ask you to be careful, I am sorry to say it, but world peace here, no, not here at all with this unrest in the heart

and still we must sing, constantly with burning tongues, come nearer earth, come nearer earth of man with your hungering eyes, let not even death do us part, throw the door wide for my love, sing in his body all people like a real place

this lie of a procession, get rid of it, this lie of a life which has come to rest in its life, get rid of it

steadily death makes its entrance through all our doors, all streets and veins, let it in, do not let it run loose, do not push it aside, but let it intervene, imply it

do not take it on your knee and look at it, but take day and night, time, even place, take them on your knee and look at us, as we open and close open and close oh—damn the procession of words

this meeting you mentioned today occurred precisely today

V

The unknown is the unknown and gold is gold I've heard, one
    winter the birds froze fast to the ice without the strength
    to scream, that's how little we can do for words with words
the books press close to one another and hold themselves up,
    backs to the living room, our buttoned-up words huddle
    on the shelf, the queue-culture of centuries, inexorably
    built up word by word, for who doesn't know that the
    word creates order
order in the lump, the formless slime, the throng of pressing
    eggs, here where we stand, order in the lumps in the throats
    of all who speak, word after word that shoves its way for-
    ward and always joins in at the right place or stumbles over
    itself, another
like that, yes, it can be said like that and the word can stop it-
    self like a letter horrified by the distance alone
but it should not be said like that, we can still see it, we can still
    see the great anonymous paper with all that Rimbaud did
    not want to write
this great unfillable white square which never has been in a
    picture by Jorn or of earth, but suddenly is there and at-
    tracts the power of all your vision
and if you go outside all the earth sings like gold in your ears
    and all their pictures rustle in your hand like our wretched
    payments
if you go outside again all this is unknown unknown and you
    can do so very little for the word your sister in this whitest
    land, a few birds left it in time
in time? —I think of a place where you lay with your head

against a root like the felled trunk

I think of a seed in your hand that you carry in memory of a
bird

I think of a green little fir still with growing tip foremost this
tingling down through the trunk,

you sit like that evening after evening, while the light burns
the words down to a flicker, darkness—are you unknown?

we walked on a stairway of snow with ice-floe hands and for-
est-edges chiming, close to each other

we flew through the house like peaks torn loose from moun-
tain massifs no one has known

see the table down there with cups and clock and the dust that
settled after our meeting

drawers, cubicles and beds, rooms full of clothes that we grew
out of or just left behind in order to die with each other

but this acquiescence is suspect, no one takes root and when
we suddenly waken in the night with a tightness: no one
will die

above us looms the whiteness, the not yet fulfilled country of
man, stretching its arms toward a sea we heard sighing
when the tiredness came

above us looms whiteness—see what we have lost, like a win-
ter

VI

I play it through to arrive at a point where the music meets re-
sistance—to get rid of the resistance and meet the music

this house is again a colossus of slag, concrete with decomposed
bits of reeds from the low factory site, mortar with im-
prints of three great hands

these blinded eyes, this vaulted conglomerate of millions of eyes
of workers from times and places—and the whip of gold
like lightning over the roof

gold, my friends, like what hung from his belt, the glowing
words that burned themselves into the middle of his body,
when the sun and he rode the desert

I have imagined Rimbaud like that, with three great hands, two
he used himself, the third used by the unknown

I have imagined music like that—oh these my two hands,
which resist finding the third

again this house where a black man opens his eyes wide as bea-
cons etching the air, where black men's blood has fertil-
ized the aged abbey brick, where a fertility woman from
a corner of the world in a corner of a temple in Mexico
bore her screams here

down in the street the snow is a dirty border around a very
common Scandinavian house with books, bath, and cen-
tral heating, with only a slight contempt left over for what
we have lost and heaped up

up here in the living room I search and search for my third
hand; perhaps, hidden by snow, it has dug its way single-
handedly, fumbled its way to the heart of this, is meeting
my resistance at the innermost center of a poem

I play this through to arrive at a point, to arrive at nothing more
    afterward, to stand still for a moment point in a house in
    a world-body, ask for a moment impossible answers for my
    questions' impossible use—then again play through this
    impossibility point by point and pause by pause, toward
    the center of time when a parting letter could easily be
    sent before 10:00 a.m. when the mailbox is emptied
but a pretty little letter that does not rummage unnecessarily
    in what has happened was already sent four years ago
I forgot to tell you about a man in a white uniform who
    walked along the street in the snow in snow-white patent
    leather shoes and ditto mustache, bouquet in slightly out-
    stretched left hand, as if nothing had happened; I thought
    he was dead
I forgot to tell you that I think of your life as of death, that I
    again and again bury your body in my body, that I again
    and again set a deadline on your luck, which will not be
    tempted, tempt my poem, which . . .
if I could begin with a scream in a temple, again in this house,
    so that they all stood risen, all were lives in your life
life, my friends, that hung from his belt and flared up, burned
    down under Africa's sun
come again, my friends, and explain it again and again—it is
    pure gold and the shining unknown like the faith of some-
    one who spoke of everything else
I think of your life, let this be innermost, let this be the center
    of my poem

VII

With my back to my poem, to myself, to my word, I go away
from myself, from my poem, from my word, and ever far-
ther into my word, into my poem, into myself

through things we arrive at things, evening and morning in
March, which is the march of days, departure upon depar-
ture, day after day, and it sounds like a procession, is one
word only, march

evening and morning, already no more point in time but the
mass of light careening in and out of itself, always the
scream, when spinal cord is divided into spinal cord by
spinal cord and all these people straighten up side by side,
horsetail ferns swaying in the morning mist, Carbonifer-
ous Period by evening as we await the glowing fire, where
the heart will begin to beat

who can think any longer of beauty, all the strangers move side
by side in the one you love, if you offer your body to him
it is the word you offer, which they do not understand—
and who dares speak anymore of the beauty of under-
standing—if you offer bread, it is the people deep under
the earth, high over the earth in mighty swaying flocks,
who say thank you, go off and sit in the chair, read the pa-
per and do not understand

but who dares speak anymore of the necessity of understanding

I walked along a street once which turned into another street
which turned into street after street I walked, I took hold
of a hand

oh country of man, oh planet whirling swallowing spitting
swinging door is someone waiting in the wings, some-
one who is bigger, bigger than evil

this door constantly winging its way between evil and good, this door that we rattle and think we have opened, which always is opened and closed by itself alone

this mill that grinds and grinds, this poem that it opens and closes like morning and evening at the same time and what I myself wanted to place like a pretty ending from one understanding to the other, I have forgotten

times, places forgotten, no longer mine, my love's, strangers', no longer, no longer words', the procession's, no longer beauty's and evil's times and places, but quite simply times and places streaming back and forth through times and places, and people winging around among people over and under endlessly back and forth

one moment forgotten all evil in the world

do not believe in the lie, do not believe in oblivion, do not believe in what is either here or there; believe in a person, perhaps a random stranger, walking forth from his strangeness, saying, I do not lie, it does not lie in me

believe that it is possible

that we have lost everything in meeting, my love—neither death nor life

with our backs to death and life we go away from death and life and farther and farther into death and life, play this terrifying theme through, I think we have mentioned it too often, in this our foreign language we have called it love, I should mention it again and again, but words do not offer the same resistance as things

not the same resistance as hearts, lock them up, let them bleed through layer after layer of consciousness, these formless bastions of the ego, where fright wanders like an imper-

sonal sheep with airy latter-day wool of spun glass as its
only hopeless defense against what?

against a not yet fulfilled country of man, which we have no
room to carry, against a house not yet built, which we have
no time to live in, against the children not yet conceived
in whom we dare not believe, write your name in their
hearts and their names in your right hand

who dares speak anymore of the necessity of understanding,
enough seen, enough owned, enough known and regard-
less of that the sun that burns and burns in the center of
your body, through the child you dream, burns it down to
a heap of sand easily whispered away like a word from your
lips

oh my pain in your life

with my back to my back I will strip my faith down to my
faith, with my back to the word, let words be words, let
lies be lies, evil be evil—do not forget, but see him drag it
behind him, the cross

believe that it is possible

who dares to speak anymore of the beauty of understanding,
who dares to speak anymore of the center of a poem, as if
it were a question of a poem, who dares to speak anymore
of the beginning, face-on, as if it were a question of meet-
ing

with our backs to our meeting we go away from our meeting
and farther and farther into our meeting, which is things'
meeting with things, which is times' and places' meeting
with time and place, which is morning and evening in
March, season and aftertime, opened and closed, at the same
time you and strangers

let me here at the brink of the whiteness, the unknown, write
a short message: to you, my love, neither life nor death, but
this word we use so often, in our foreign language we have
called it love.

Letter in April

There are the landscapes we have traveled through and lived in, which have seldom been the same ones at the same time.

There is the way consciousness carries those landscapes forward, and their transformation into a perceptible space where vastly different places grow together.

There is our work with images, words, to bring all things back to the landscape they come from. Which has been the same one at the same time all along.

I

○ ○ ○ ○ ○

We arrive early one morning,
almost before we're awake.
The air is pale, a bit cool,
and it curls a bit over our skin
like a membrane of moisture.
We talk about spiderwebs
—how do they work—
about the rain that washed the water
as we slept along the way
while we rolled
over the earth.
Then we're at the house
and we bathe in the dust of the gravel walk
as among sparrows.

○ ○ ○ ○

Is this waterfall
of images
really a house.
Is it really we
who will live
here, plunging
through the multitude
of gods.
Live, set the table,
and share.

o

Unpacking our belongings,
some jewelry
a few playthings
paper,
the necessities
arranged within
the world
for a while.
And while you draw,
mapping out
whole continents
between the bed
and table,
the labyrinth turns,

hanging suspended,
and the thread
that never leads out
is, for a moment,
outside.

∘ ∘

Then light pours
in suddenly
and hides us completely.
The sun is round
as the apple is green
and they rise and they fall.

∘ ∘ ∘

Already on the street
with our money clutched
in our hands
and the world is a white bakery
where we waken too early
and dream too late
where streams of raw
and unused thoughts
come nearest the truth
long before they are thought.

II

○ ○ ○

Uneasy doves everywhere
and fear of the poem
that flies up
in alarm
at the least
movement.
Scattering breadcrumbs
so the words will
settle.
Soon
just a pecking
remains
at the least
little crumb
of meaning,
sentenceless
and cruel.
Soon just
a natural
violent peace.

○ ○

Then light pours
in suddenly
and screams
past itself
when we are born.

But more meaninglessly
and beautifully
as in an afterimage
of sorrow,
eyes listen
to the light,
which is white and flows
like milk.
And as we drink
we hear thirst
slaked.

ooooo

Walking out onto the terrace,
while twilight opens its floodgates
and everything slips into oneness
with itself.
And what you asked
about the spiderweb,
and the rain washing the water,
maybe,
but I don't exactly know
if dew can be remembered.
The dew that in summer
velveted the web as soft
as only a wonder can be
and taught us what work was,
that it was
like the word dew,
and if you read its mirror image,
like god.

ooo o

All forgiven,
what I thought,
and gave back
to the world
again.
This house
like a shell
kissed thin
and without wonder.
Sound carries only
as a murmur
through the mass of leaves
in a whole different place,
on a tree
that someone else looks at
in the distance,
maybe from a bus
standing still.

o

Meanwhile winter and summer
and winter again
spent in the company
of something as simple
as a completely
worldless
pomegranate
that says
nothing.

And as you sleep
and map out
whole continents
along sleep-river
shores,
I unwrap the pomegranate
from its purple paper
and slice it
in half.
It looks like
a kind of brain
different from ours.
Who knows,
maybe the pomegranate
itself is aware
that it's called
something else.
Who knows,
maybe I myself
am called
something else
than myself.

I think,
therefore I am part
of the labyrinth.
Words of comfort,
hope of escape.
There is only the river
with its two great shores.
On one,
a tale, an idyll
and raging hope
for explanation
and end.
On the other
the one and only explanation
that spreads
and spreads
and spreads
into
itself.

III

○

That's how it's so still in the silence here.
It's a bit like the sound in a lightbulb
when the filament burns out,
but the light is not even on.
Just still, and the rain from before,
which my ear can't exactly remember,
distilled, dated,
and worldless.

○○○○

Only remnants of an electric whisper
in the house,
while of its own accord the room
holds still and waits
for my letter.
Dear vanished wonder,
I must create my own wonder
or come under the sway
of the same vanishing
in language
as later in death.
Without understanding
and without comparing.

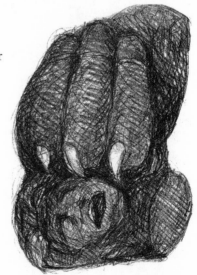

ooo

On the street again,
and over the gate a head
with wide-open mouth
swallowing every word
that is said.
And while this staring
stone figure
regards us
with the same
passionate apathy
needed
to repeat the world,
we walk
with the greatest
precision
between dove droppings
and dead vagrants
who breathe,
as if we were
respecting
the gathered
ragged freedom
by breaking
the last
introspective link
and being forced
to translate
everything back
into itself.

That's how, in the yard
every night as we sleep,
a palm tree stands.

∘ ∘

The palm tree is strong
as the wind is green.
The rage we once
called holy.
The language that once
had a direction.
The future that once
rebounded
onto us.

The indifference now
that I myself have come along
around the sun
forty-four times.
The indifference now
that the closed cycle
opens its doors.
The indifference
in this insufferable
image of reality.
Teach me to repeat
the future now,
while we are being born.
Let my mind fly up
into its nest
in the depths
of the rustling crown.
Let the eggs shine

with an afterglow
like milky sun.
Let the wind be green
and sorrow slaked.

ooooo

But I don't exactly know;
maybe
it's many miles
to the nearest spider.
We set off, and long
before the sun rises
we're outside the town.
And here, as we walk on our way,
going along
with the earth,
which moves in its own
slightly rolling way
like animals
through fog,
our minds are
spun
like a world
around us.

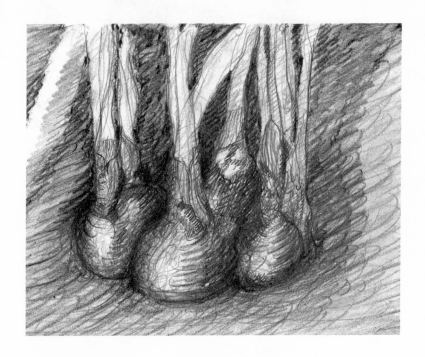

IV

ooooo

So here we sit
in this violent solitude,
where bulbs work
underground,
and we wait.
Around noon
when the mountain rain stops,
a bird stands
on a stone.
Around evening

when the heart stands empty,
a woman stands
in the road.
Her face
is wrinkled and round
and it looks
as if she is remembering
herself back
in time
while silently
figuring
when
and why
she might have last
seen a human being.
She nods
and leaves.

○ ○

I see the wood anemones.
I don't imagine
that the anemones
see me
but still there is,
while they oxidize
the forest air
and in the crumbling
afterimage
as after burning
magnesium,
something that tells me
I am more visible

○

Tell me
that things
speak
their own
clear
language.

○ ○ ○ ○

The stone lion with eyes
blind as bulbs
underground
that carries
the foundation of the house
and the cellar's undermost

slipping depths,
where aged babies
whimper like motherless
monks and nuns,
and stone vines,
fragments of leaves
of the raging
passionate cold,
unraveling
from the ragged mouth
of the underworld,
the mouth mute and cross
almost like some odd
exhibit
sloshing the whole world's

cultures
into the light
like a sow
farrowing.
All this whispering
through the multitude
of membranes
and skin,
all this human
commotion
we are forced to call
delight, and be delighted
joy, and rejoice

pleasure, bliss, blessing, happiness,
and like a swift
asleep in air
house our homeless
sanity in a dream.

o o o

Already on the street
with our money clutched
in our hands,
and the world is a white laundry,
where we are boiled and wrung
and dried and ironed,
and slicked down
and forsaken
we sweep
back
in children's dreams
of chains and jail
and the heartfelt sigh
of liberation,
and in the spark trails
of feelings
the fire eater
the cigarette swallower
come
to light
and we pay
and distance ourselves
with laughter.

V

○ ○ ○

A caring
like what is needed
to repeat the world.
This daily arrival
in all kinds of guises
of all that is
evident,
chaste and sexual
in one.
The monster's
lovely dream
of wandering
among human
caresses.
The kiss
beneath moist
vaults
whose seeds
look like
a landscape in the brain.
And if we didn't know better,
we would take a walk
in ourselves
and meet there.

o o o o

Little sensible dream,
when evening after evening
in my bed
I count beds,
how many
and where
I have slept
in my life,
and in all these places
as I slept
I dreamed
a dream
that evening after evening
draws near
to the same place
even in the chalk chambers

of hospitals
dreamed it
and in the morning
only the remnant of an electric whisper
when the bouquet is carried in.

∘∘∘∘∘

Setting out on
the network of roads
in darkness,
when the way home
is longer
and the stars
broadcast
on the blue-white
road signs'
wavelengths.
Now and then
turnouts,
pockets of light.
A man
with a basket
that's empty.
A girl
in windbreaker
and helmet
and on her cheek
a bit of dried salt
from her windblown
eyes.

And here on our way
going along
with the earth,
which is evidently going along
in its own
slightly rolling way
with a sun
that long ago
vanished,
it happens that everything
of its own accord
slips into
your hand in mine,
and lines from
an atlas
of eternal presence
spread
and spread
and spread
like a homecoming
in the body.
And as we cross
the river,
you say
that we're crossing
the river.
While the violent
solitude
opens its floodgates.

∘ ∘

It's so easy,
as easy as anything
in April
it's actually
just walking
there in the forest
as we did then
as easy
as if it were
not a thing in the world
in April
to walk there
as we did then
with each other

hand in hand
really nothing
to speak of
in the anemone breeze
as if we never
had separated
from each other
as easy
as anything
in April
because they wither
so fast
and in the oxidized
forest air
the pine is fire
as the text is wild.

o

So easy, child's play
as in another
kind of brain
here
on the blazing
playground
here
where everyone
at the noon hour
opens
the closed city
here

where the hottest battles
the razed hopes
imitate joy
and its sharp
breathing.
Who knows,
maybe joy itself
is aware
that it's called
something else
here
where it all
breathes an idyll.
This is how
as I sit
here on the bench
wreathed in the world's
freest breaths,
and the sounds blessedly
boil over
in another kind
of silence,
so warm,
and half asleep
so dusty
that the river dries out,
I cross it dryshod,
and in the desert
I stop
beneath the fruit pyramid,

and sniff.
It is guarded
by a dog
with wheels
beneath its paralyzed
hind legs.
And there
between the lumpy
forepaws
lies the shining
pomegranate
which I otherwise
so very silently
would have forgotten.

VI

o

Silent, but nothing to find
in the precious silence.
Only an echo of frost
like a cackle.
An overwintering fly that waits
but no one who turns on the light.
Inroad
in a world of outcomes,
impulse
in a world of expulsions,
joy
in a world of ancient
jails,
the pleasure of random events guided
by deft need,
boundaries for everything,
and suffocation
in a dead
furor.
Now and then a lone
worldless person
who turns on a light
in his cave
and the fly that dies
with melted
wings
at once,

just a crackle,
just an echo of frost,
when the body
is brushed away.
And yet
if all
that our eyes follow,
if things
have it right,
then freedom exists,
but all
its details
are faster
than light
and arrive
from the real
reigning order,
which we so stubbornly
consider
chaos
before we begin
to speak.
That's how
every
revolution is
when it first
breaks out,
a disguised
revelation,
a joy

in what is outside
that never
manages to repeat
the world
inside
of words,
because our wonder
grows too strong
and is called fear.
Who knows,
maybe death itself
is aware
that it's called
something else.

○ ○

A sorrow
that speaks
in clusters
of concealing
light.
So simply that light
gets the eye to see
that it is light
in the rustling
darkness.
So simply
that light is as fast
as the eye is a hole.
So easily

when the closed cycle
opens its doors,
as easily as anything,
as in the distant
acacias'
glowing
grave mounds,
the world
so killed
and buried
then and there
in light,
light
that stands still,
so easily

in April
in the April
of pain
when acacias
see me
as my mother did
when I was born.
And while I draw
and map out
whole continents
between kin
and sorrow,
the revolution turns,
hanging suspended,
and the feeling
that never leads out
is for a moment
outside
itself
and illuminated
in the dead,
inconsolable
visible
and the silence
has doors everywhere.

o o o

Inconsolable
visible
as caring

and doing,
women's
long
remembering,
caresses
and kisses
in another
kind of language
that is signs'
own.
That's how
every night as we sleep
like bread
that comes nearest
the truth,
that's how
every day as we glow
like raw and unused
sheets,
the world is repeated
in the world
of repetition,
the courageous
goodness
of things.
Bread that is eaten,
and when eaten
becomes concern.
Sleep that is slept
and when slept becomes soft

as a chain is broken.
Almost
like a turn
in the weather,
a joyous,
tough rhetoric,
and each
revolution
in silence.

∘∘∘∘

Solemn
clear
foaming
rage
and its fragments
under the sway
of the same vanishing
in death
as my wonder
in language.
This harrowing
that must devour
the harrowed
world
again
while food
stands untouched,
almost like an odd
exhibit,
for show.

That's how I've dreamed
a mortal dream
that evening after evening
draws near to a place
that is always
the same,
a shell
kissed thin
and when it breaks
the boundary spreads
to what
it always
has been,
a waterfall

of images,
really,
a house
through the multitude
that lives, demonstrates,
shares,
so fully visible
to a wondering world.

ooooo

With, as language,
not a trace
other than the sky,
no beating
with clenched
fists,
only the poem
that freely
unfolds
the future
like a parachute
of silk and silence,
a fan
of shifted lighting,
passionate
star-sent
unyielding
indifference
spun
into mind

as we go
in our own
slightly rolling way
around the sun.
Then we're at the house.

VII

ooooo

We make it as fine
as we can.
We bathe,
clean house,
sweep the spider
down,
and when the rain
stops
we go out
onto the terrace
and listen
to the river.
On the road
a woman walks
past,
and just
to the left
of the sprouting bulbs
a bird

sits
on a stone.
And all evening
beneath the stars'
light
we study
the map,
your hand
in mine
and our bodies
in the house.

○ ○ ○ ○

Setting the table
the next morning
in the shade
by the stone
lion.
Scrubbing the foundation
with water
from the splashing
fountain.
Straightening up
the innermost
cellar,
and putting the fruit
in place,
sorted,
in order.
At lunchtime

the sound
of a baby
crying
in the neighbors' yard.
At dinnertime
the bus
at last
holding still
in the distance.
A swift
circles
in the air
above the house
and the sound
of the eternal
waterfall
rises and falls
in the fountain
which you draw
so that it looks like
a bouquet being carried in.

o

Bringing up fruit
from the fruit pyramid
in the cellar.
Slicing it
in half
and we eat.
Leaving the pomegranate

there on my desk.
Snipping purple paper
into playthings
and winding the thread
back onto the spool,
the thread that you pretended
was a complicated
web
between the bed
and table.
Going out
to the nearest
playground,
where last time
there was a dog
better
at soccer
than the boys
themselves.
At night
your sharp
breathing,
the sound
of the small
belongings
scattered around,
the sound
of myself
and my clothes,
as I write a poem
on the back of a drawing

that represents something
I can't see.

o o

Opening the doors,
it's cool,
April,
getting milk,
boiling eggs,
and searching
the newspaper
for the date,
the weather forecast,
all the names
in the foreign
death announcements.
The earth is
completely white
with sun
and flies up
at the least thing.
And I tell
you again
about the anemones.
About how
we lay in the anemones
as children.
And you're not sure you
remember
whether what you really

remember
is the anemones
from last time.
And we talk about
the pine
in the middle of the yard.
Maybe what it remembers
is the wind.
Maybe what it remembers
is the sound.
A place
between
pine
wind
and fire.

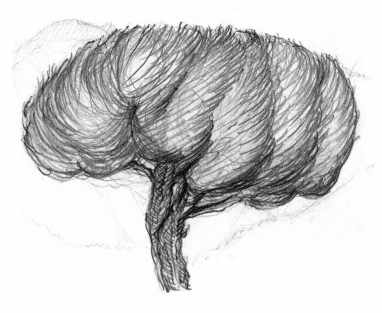

○ ○ ○

On the street
with our money
clutched
in our hands,
buying bread
and scattering breadcrumbs
for the bluish
doves.
Paying
to see
the fire eater
the cigarette swallower
and the dead vagrant
who breathes.
Greeting
the palm tree
that rustles
at night.
Saying a few words
to the staring
stone figure
above the gate.
Laughing
and rushing
in
as if chased.
In the cool kitchen
we prepare
and arrange our food.

We make it as fine
as we can.
Bouquet on the table
and all.
And we speak
in our own
clear
language.
Who knows,
maybe things themselves
are aware
that we're called
something else.

NOTES

p. 10   Aksel Sandemose (1899–1965) was a Danish/Norwegian author.

p. 43   The Danish equivalent of "Ladybug, ladybug, fly away home" is a children's rhyme urging the ladybug (associated, as in English, with Mary, mother of Jesus) to "fly to Our Lord" and "pray for good weather tomorrow."

p. 57   In the standard Danish Lutheran funeral liturgy, the pastor sprinkles a handful of earth onto the coffin, saying, "Dust thou art, unto dust shalt thou return, and from dust shalt thou again arise."

p. 75   A gossip mirror is a small mirror attached to the outside of a window frame on the front of a house. The mirror is angled so that a person sitting indoors can follow comings and goings in the street.

p. 78   The Danish word for "promise" is *love*. To "cross out promise," drawing a line through it, creates the Danish word *løve*, "lion."

p. 107 The Danish word for "dew" is *dug*. Its mirror image would be *gud*, "god."

p. 138 Christensen alludes to lines from Stéphane Mallarmé's "ÉVENTAIL de Madame Mallarmé" (*Stéphane Mallarmé: Oeuvres Complètes*. Ed. Henri Mondor and G. Jean-Aubry. Paris: Gallimard, 1945.):

> Avec comme pour langage
> Rien qu'un battement aux cieux
> Le future vers se dégage
> Du logis très précieux

An English translation by E. H. and A. M. Blackmore, "Madame Mallarmé's Fan" in *Stéphane Mallarmé: Collected Poems* (Oxford: Oxford University Press, 2006):

> With no language but a trace
> just a beating in the skies
> so this future verse will rise
> from its precious dwelling-place